THE
VIKINGS

ROSEMARY REES

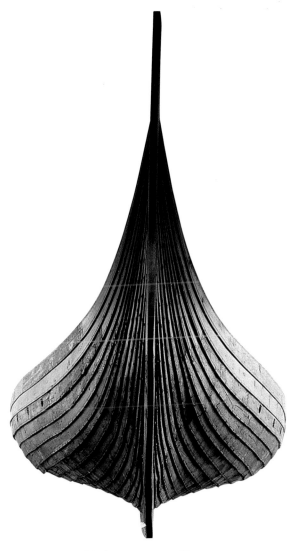

Heinemann Library
Chicago, Illinois

© 2002 Reed Educational & Professional Publishing
Published by Heinemann Library,
an imprint of Reed Educational & Professional Publishing,
Chicago, Illinois

Customer Service 888-454-2279

Visit our website at www.heinemannlibrary.com

Designed by Depke Design
Map illustrations by John Fleck
Color illustrations by Martin Smillie
Printed and bound in the United States by Lake Book Manufacturing, Inc.

06 05 04 03 02
10 9 8 7 6 5 4 3 2 1

Library of Congress Cataloging-in-Publication Data
Rees, Rosemary, 1942-
  The Vikings / Rosemary Rees.
    p. cm. -- (Understanding people in the past)
Includes index.
Summary: Presents an overview of the ancient Vikings, discussing such
topics as travel, work, family life, food, entertainment, buildings,
religion, farming, and art.
  ISBN 1-58810-422-2 (HC), 1-4034-0100-4 (Pbk.)
  1. Vikings--Juvenile literature. [1. Vikings.] I. Title. II. Series.
  DL65 .R44 2002
  948'.022--dc21
                              2001005324

Acknowledgments
The author and publisher are grateful to the following for permission to reproduce copyright material:

Cover photograph courtesy of Bibliotheque Nationale de France.

Title page, p 59 Art Resource/Werner Forman Archive; pp. 5, 8, 10, 13B, 16, 17, 18, 21, 25, 27L, 29, 32, 33, 35T, 47R,
48, 56 C M Dixon; p 23T University Museum of Cultural Heritage, University of Oslo; pp. 6, 7B, 22, 23B, 36L York
Archaeological Trust for Excavation and Research Ltd; p. 7T The Viking Ship Museum in Roskilde; pp. 9, 14, 49R The
National Heritage Board, Stockholm; p. 12 Statens Historiska Museum; p. 15 National Museum of Iceland/Werner
Forman Archive; pp. 20, 28 Michael Holford; pp. 24, 43B National Museum of Denmark; p. 27R Stofnun Arna
Magnussonar, Iceland; p. 31 Museum of National Antiquities, Stockholm; p. 35B Statens Historiska Museum; pp.
36R, 37T, 37B, 39, 42 University Museum of Cultural Heritage, University of Oslo; p. 44 The Royal Library, National
Library of Sweden; pp. 45, 54 Corbis; p. 50 Scottish Viewpoint; p. 52 Institut Amatller D'art Hispanic; pp. 26, 58 Art
Resource/Werner Forman Archive/National Museum of Copenhagen, Denmark

Every effort has been made to contact copyright holders of any material reproduced in this book.
Any omissions will be rectified in subsequent printings if notice is given to the publisher.

Some words are shown in bold, **like this.** You can find out what they
mean by looking in the glossary.

Contents

Who Were the Vikings?

The Vikings lived in northeast Europe and Scandinavia more than a thousand years ago. They were people who came from the countries we now call Norway, Denmark, and Sweden. At first, these people were called Norsemen, Northmen, or Danes. *Norse* was the Norwegian word for "north." The word "viking" was used to describe what the Norsemen did. It probably came from the word *Vik* which means to fight as a pirate or warrior. The word was soon used to describe the people, too.

Historians and **archaeologists** have found out that Vikings were farmers, **traders,** and **settlers** as well as pirates, warriors, and explorers.

This map shows the Vikings' homelands and the places where they settled.

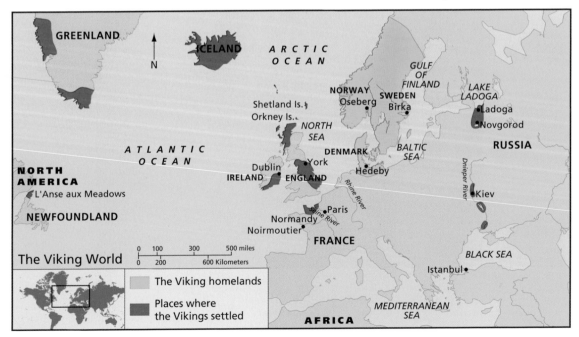

The Viking World

0 100 300 500 miles
0 200 600 Kilometers

The Viking homelands

Places where the Vikings settled

GREENLAND
ICELAND
ARCTIC OCEAN
GULF OF FINLAND
NORWAY
SWEDEN
Oseberg
Birka
LAKE LADOGA
Ladoga
Novgorod
Shetland Is.
Orkney Is.
NORTH SEA
ATLANTIC OCEAN
DENMARK
BALTIC SEA
RUSSIA
NORTH AMERICA
Dublin
York
IRELAND
ENGLAND
Hedeby
Rhine River
Dnieper River
Kiev
L'Anse aux Meadows
NEWFOUNDLAND
Normandy
Paris
Seine River
Noirmoutier
FRANCE
BLACK SEA
Istanbul
MEDITERRANEAN SEA
AFRICA

Viking pirates and raiders

The Vikings began terrorizing towns and cities in Europe from about 793. People everywhere prayed, "God, deliver us from the fury of the Northmen."

Vikings sailed up rivers and **raided** cities, burning whatever they did not take with them. The Vikings raided mainly to get cattle and horses, food, and valuable gold and silver objects. They became known for their surprise attacks and quick retreats.

Viking sailors and traders

The Vikings were skilled ship builders and navigators. Vikings from Norway sailed to Iceland, Greenland, and North America. Danish Vikings settled in Belgium, the Netherlands, France, and England. Vikings from Sweden sailed up Russian rivers to great trading centers like the cities of Kiev on the Dneiper River and Bolga on the Volga River.

The Vikings made jewelry from bronze and silver. This silver brooch shows an animal and a snake twisted around each other.

How Do We Know About the Vikings?

Archaeologists have uncovered many clues about the Vikings. They find out where the Vikings lived and where they went to as **raiders, settlers,** and **traders.** Then they dig in the ground at different **sites** and **excavate** buried objects, called **artifacts,** that once belonged to the Vikings. Artifacts give archaeologists clues about how the Vikings lived and also help them build a picture of life during Viking times.

Some sites, like the one at Coppergate in York, England, are very difficult to excavate. This is because they have been built over by other people since the time of the Vikings.

These archaeologists are working at Coppergate, York, in 1981. They found the remains of wooden houses and workshops. They found over 30,000 objects such as glass beads, knives, **amber** pendants, metal brooches, keys, and coins. They also found leather boots, shoes, wooden cups, and bowls.

This is a photograph of an underwater excavation. In 1956, part of a Viking ship was found in shallow water at Roskilde, Denmark. A dam was built around the ship in 1962 and the water was drained out to aid the excavation. Archaeologists eventually found five ships on the site.

Other sites are easier to excavate. Some sites, like Hedeby in Denmark, were abandoned by the Vikings and now lie under farmland. Thus, there are no buildings or roads to dig around or through.

Looking for artifacts is just part of an archaeologist's work. They have to write down everything they find and mark where they found it. They also have to measure and photograph everything they find. They clean up small finds, like coins, jewelry, leather, cloth, and wood and preserve them. They study soil samples and find the remains of seeds, insects, and animal bones. In these ways, they create a picture of what it was like to live in Viking times.

These are some Viking artifacts found by archaeologists. There are combs made from deer antlers and pins made from animal bones.

Evidence in Pictures and Words

Clues from carvings

Some clues about Viking life come from carvings in stone and wood. Wood carvings at a church in Norway show a sword being made and meat being cooked. Other wood carvings have shown ships in full sail and men fishing. Stone carvings often have messages cut in **runes,** which are the letters Vikings used for writing.

These are wood carvings from a church in Hylestad, Norway. They tell stories about Sigurd the Dragon-slayer. They also give us clues about what Viking swords looked like, what Vikings wore, and how they cooked.

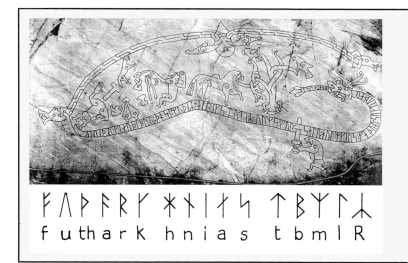

futhark hnias tbmlR

Runes

Vikings used runes when they wrote. Runes were letters made from straight lines. There were sixteen runes and the Vikings called them *futhark.* Vikings carved runes into wood, stone, and metal. At first, they thought runes were magic. Later, runes were used on memorial stones.

The picture on the left is of a memorial stone in Ramsund, Sweden. The runes carved in the dragon's body say, "Sigrid built this bridge in memory of her husband, Holmger. (She) was Orm's daughter."

Clues from tapestries

Woven pictures, or **tapestries,** made by the Vikings give us clues about their lives. **Archaeologists** found a tapestry in a ship burial at Oseberg, Norway. It shows the type of clothes the Vikings wore and the transportation they used on land.

Clues in words

Carving runes into stone or wood took a long time, so Vikings just told and re-told their poems, stories, and histories. By the end of the 1100s, Vikings in Iceland learned to write on **vellum.** This was much quicker. They wrote the history of the first 400 **settlers** there. They called it the *Landnamabok.* Later, they wrote Viking adventure stories, called **sagas.** Other people, like Arab **traders,** wrote about the Vikings, too.

Society and Government

Viking society

Vikings were divided into three groups. *Jarls* were the **nobles.** They were rich and powerful landowners. A *jarl* might become the leader of a district and sometimes a king over many districts.

Karls were the largest group of people. They were born free and so were their children. *Karls* could be farmers, **merchants,** or others who served the ruler or worked for themselves. A *karl* who was very poor, had no family to help him, and had no land on which to grow food could volunteer to become a *thrall.*

Thralls were slaves and so were their children. They owned nothing and had no rights. They worked for *jarls* and *karls.* Prisoners taken from battle could also become *thralls.* It was possible for a *thrall* to work very hard and buy freedom for himself and his family.

Viking government

Viking freemen held open-air meetings, called *Things* to settle disputes. They discussed problems about land ownership,

This is Tynwald Hill in the Isle of Man, off the coast of England. A Viking *Thing* met here every summer to settle disputes. Only men could vote. They brought their families. There was a market and a fair. People arranged marriages and passed on their news.

divorce, robbery, and murder. Vikings also made laws and decided whether the community would go to war. Districts had their own *Things* and their own sets of laws.

Vikings in Iceland had one *Thing* for the whole island. It was called the *Althing* and met for two weeks at midsummer each year. A Viking who would not accept the rulings of the *Althing* became an outlaw. He lost his belongings and his land. Anyone could kill him without fear of punishment.

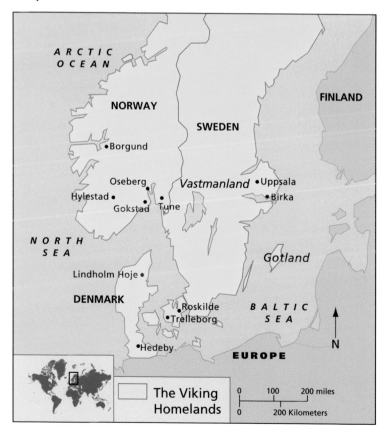

In Viking times the boundaries between Norway, Sweden, and Denmark were not firmly fixed. Vikings lived mainly where the land was **fertile.**

What Did the Vikings Wear?

Viking pictures, **tapestries,** and **sagas** teach us a lot about Viking men, women, and children. They tell us, for example, about their clothes and what they looked like.

Men's clothes

Men wore long pants that reached to their knees or ankles. Their pants were usually held up by a sash or drawstring. Men also wore tunics made from brown or green cloth. On special occasions, they wore tunics edged with gold and silver thread and had silk headbands to hold back their hair.

Women's clothes

Women wore long, pleated wool or linen dresses with a tunic over the top. They fastened their tunics to straps using brooches. On a chain hanging down from their brooches, women would have a knife, comb, key, and needles. Sometimes they might wear a shawl over their tunic. For special occasions, their dresses were made from silk.

Men and women wore flat leather shoes and thick wool socks. In the winter they wore fur or wool hats and warm cloaks fastened at the

This is a Viking pendant. It shows a woman with long hair. She is wearing a shawl over a dress with pleats at the back. Her long hair falls loosely from a knot at the back of her head. The beads on her chest probably hang from her shoulder brooches.

These are the sort of clothes a Viking farmer and his wife would have worn. They dressed to be comfortable and so styles did not change much throughout the Viking period.

shoulder with a brooch or pin. On special occasions they wore rings and bracelets and they used eye make-up, too.

Making clothes

Vikings made their everyday clothes from wool and linen cloth. They used vegetable dyes to make the cloth blue, red, green, brown, black, or yellow. Vikings made their special occasion clothes from silk and brocades, brought back from China and the Far East by **traders.**

A Viking woman wore this brooch on one of her shoulders to hold her tunic to its straps.

Family Life

Family loyalties

A Viking family consisted of parents and children, uncles and aunts, grandparents, and cousins. Family members were often more loyal to each other than to their leaders. This sometimes led to fights, or **feuds,** between families.

Feuds usually happened when someone in one family killed a person in another. The dead person's family took revenge. This led to more killings. Sometimes families took their feud to the *Thing.* Members of the *Thing* decided who was right and who was wrong.

This is a **runestone** from Sweden. It was carved about 1,000 years ago. A farmer had it made in memory of his wife. One sentence on it says: "No better wife will come to Hassmyra to look after the farm."

Marriage and divorce

Viking women were treated with respect. If they wanted to marry, they could choose their own husband and keep their own property after they were married. When their husbands were away fighting or **trading,** the wives ran the house.

Marriages often took place in the early winter, when everyone was home. When marriages went wrong, divorces were easy to get. The husband or wife wanting the divorce simply had to make a formal statement in front of witnesses, and the marriage was over.

Children

A father showed that his newborn baby was accepted into the family by picking it up and wrapping it in his cloak.

Small children lived at home with their parents. Older children were sometimes sent to live with foster parents. This made bonds between certain families stronger, which helped if there were family feuds.

Children learned the skills they would need when they were adults. Girls learned to cook, spin, weave, sew, milk cows, and make butter and cheese. They helped weed the fields and look after the animals. Boys learned how to hunt, fish, and work on the farm. Both boys and girls learned to ride, swim, and fight.

The Vikings played board games. This one was called *hnefatafl.* It was like chess—the "king" had to be protected from attack by the pieces of the other player.

Gods and Goddesses

Where did the gods and goddesses live?

Vikings believed that their gods and goddesses lived in Asgard. They were all members of two families, called the Asir and the Vanir, who had once been at war.

A rainbow bridge called Bifrost joined Asgard to Midgard, where people lived. All around Midgard was an ocean full of monsters. Beyond this ocean was Utgard, where the Frost Giants lived. These giants were enemies of the gods.

Vikings believed that if they died in battle, women called Valkyries took them to **Valhalla.** Valhalla was a great hall in Asgard. It belonged to Odin, the greatest Viking god.

What happened after death?

Many Vikings believed that a person's spirit sailed off to a new life, so some Viking kings and queens were buried in ships. Most Vikings were buried with food for the journey and useful objects to help them in their next life. Many ordinary people had stones set around their graves in the shape of a ship.

This silver charm is in the shape of Thor's hammer.

Odin, Thor, and Frey

Odin was the king of all the Norse gods and goddesses. He knew the magic of the **runes** and was the god of poets, kings, *jarls,* and magicians. Each night he hunted with his eight-legged horse and his two wolves. His two pet ravens flew all over the world and returned each night to tell Odin what they had seen and heard.

Thor was the most popular Viking god. He was large and strong, with a bright red beard and a quick temper. When he rode across the sky in his chariot, he made the thunder rumble. He used his hammer, Mjöllni, in battles with the Frost Giants. His job was to protect the gods and goddesses from the giants. He was always having adventures and the Vikings loved telling stories about him.

Frey was another popular Viking god. He was the god of love and marriage. Frey also ruled the rain and sunshine, which made the crops grow. His twin sister Freyja, was the goddess of love and fertility. She helped women during childbirth.

This small bronze statue of Thor was found in Iceland. Thor was the god of thunder and lightning.

Living on the Land

Animals and crops

Viking farmers kept cattle, sheep, goats, pigs, and hens. They grew vegetables like cabbages and onions and probably had apple trees, too. They grew crops like oats, barley, wheat, and rye. The fields had stone walls around them to keep the animals out. They cut grass to dry so the animals had hay to eat in the winter. The animals and crops provided the Vikings with leather, wool, and bone for shoes and clothes, blankets, and drinking cups, as well as food.

Farms and farmhouses

The main building of a Viking farm was the **longhouse.** It could be up to 98 feet (30 meters) long. At first, animals and people lived in the

Vikings in Iceland built their houses from blocks of earth and grass because there was very little wood and stone there. This same material was used for the roof, too.

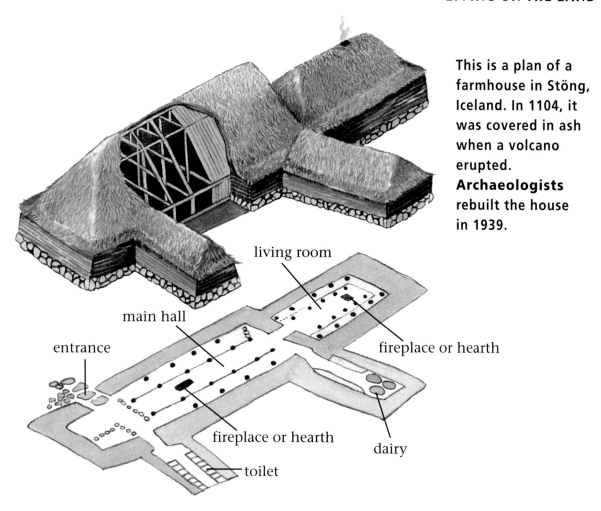

This is a plan of a farmhouse in Stöng, Iceland. In 1104, it was covered in ash when a volcano erupted. **Archaeologists** rebuilt the house in 1939.

living room

main hall

entrance

fireplace or hearth

fireplace or hearth

dairy

toilet

same building. Later, Vikings built separate barns and storage areas for their animals and tools.

How do we know?

We know about Viking farms from **sagas** and **excavations**. Photographs from the air show patterns of Viking fields and buried buildings that cannot be seen from the ground. Some Viking farms are still farms today.

The Farming Year

Who did the work?
On small farms, all the work was done by the farmer and his family. On larger farms, *karls* and *thralls* helped, too.

Spring
In spring, the fields were plowed, seeds sown, and vegetables planted. When this was done, the Viking farmer went **raiding,** leaving his wife in charge.

Summer
Vikings grew hay and **fodder** crops to feed the animals through the winter. They took the cattle and sheep to the high pastures, called *shielings.* There the animals ate the fresh grass, leaving the grass around the farm to be kept for winter hay.

Farming scenes woven into this **tapestry** from 1092 show what Viking farming would have been like.

The summer months in Iceland

The six months of summer were named after the work done on the farm at that time:

Cuckoo month or sowing time—mid April to mid May
Egg time or lamb's fold time—mid May to mid June
Shieling month or sun month—mid June to mid July
Haymaking month—mid July to mid August
Corn-cutting month—mid August to mid September
Autumn month—mid September to mid October

Fall

The farmer came back to work on the farm in the fall. Everyone was busy harvesting the crops. The grain was used to make beer or ground into flour. The weakest animals were killed and their meat was salted, smoked, or dried so that it could be eaten in the winter.

Winter

Viking winters were long, dark, and cold, so most of the work was done inside. Vikings made shoes, harnesses, and sleeping bags from animal skins; they made and mended tools and equipment; and they repaired their boats, ready for another year.

This ax head was found in Denmark. It is made from iron and decorated with silver.

Inside a Longhouse

The building

The outside walls of a **longhouse** could be made from wood, stone, or turf. The inside walls were usually made from wood. The floor was hard-packed earth, covered with reed plants. The roof was held up by two rows of wooden posts. The roof had a hole in the middle for smoke to escape. Some houses had windows. There was no glass, but shutters could be pulled across the openings.

The rooms

The first longhouses had just one room. Later, separate rooms were added. There might be a bedroom, a room for spinning and weaving, a kitchen, and a dairy. Benches were built into the walls and used as seats during

This is a reconstruction of a Viking house in York, England. It shows the hearth as the family meeting place.

the day and beds at night. However, the room where the fire was, the *skali,* was always the most important. Meals were eaten there and guests entertained.

Heat and light

When it was dark, some light came from the fire. Small bowls holding burning oil were hung from the roof or attached to the walls. Vikings hung **tapestries** on their walls for decoration and to keep out drafts. Vikings slept on straw-filled mattresses under wool blankets and sheepskin rugs. They had pillows and quilts filled with feathers, too.

Archaeologists found this wooden bed in the Oseberg ship burial in Norway. Whoever owned it was probably important because ordinary people did not own beds.

Viking women spun wool and wove it into cloth almost daily.

Cooking and Eating

Food

Vikings ate fish like cod, haddock, and herring. They kept pigs and sheep for meat and hunted deer, boar, reindeer, seals, and whales. Farmers also kept chickens, geese, and ducks for meat and for their eggs.

Vikings grew cabbages, onions, peas, raspberries, plums, and cherries. They also grew barley, rye, and oats. They ground the grain into flour to make bread and made a kind of porridge. They made beer, wine, and **mead.** They drank milk, too, and made it into butter, cheese, and yogurt. Vikings grew garlic and flavored their food with spices brought by **traders** from markets in the East.

Vikings boiled meat and simmered stews in iron cauldrons. They baked meat and bread in deep pits filled with red-hot coals. Some Viking homes had a stone oven built into the wall.

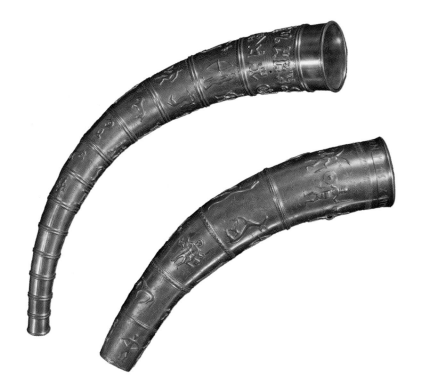

Vikings drank beer from drinking horns that were usually made from hollowed out cows' horns. Rich Vikings had drinking horns made from gold with silver decorations.

Mealtimes

Vikings ate twice a day: at about eight o'clock in the morning and at about seven o'clock in the evening. The meal was put on a long table and the Viking family sat around it on wooden benches or on a type of folding chair. They ate from wooden plates and bowls with wooden spoons and iron knives. There were no forks.

How do we know?

Archaeologists have studied bones and seeds in Viking settlements. They found food and kitchen equipment in the Oseberg ship burial in Norway, as well.

Feasting and Fun

Feasts

Vikings had three great religious feasts each year that they celebrated in every district and wherever Vikings were outside their homelands. The feast of *Sigrblot* was at the beginning of summer; *Vetrarblot* was after the harvest; and *Jolablot* was after mid-winter. *Blot* means "sacrifice" and at each feast a horse was sacrificed to the gods. At that time, the Vikings asked for good harvests, mild winters, and victory in battle. Then there was great feasting. The horse was roasted and eaten, and there was pork and beef to eat, too. The Vikings drank strong ale and **mead.**

Rich Vikings ate off silver plates and drank from silver cups with white linen cloths on their tables. People put on their best clothes and traveled miles to feast at the homes of friends and relatives.

Poetry

Poets, called *skalds,* made up new verses and retold old poems. These poems often contained *kennings,* or word games. People told riddles and jokes, listened to old **sagas,** and made up new ones.

The best *skalds* traveled around, making up verses. This silver arm band was given to a *skald* for a really good poem.

They got themselves ready for the raid and set off for the town. The men of the town had seen them coming, however, and decided to fight them. There was a wooden wall built round the town to protect it. Men were sent to stand on this wall and defend the town against the Vikings. A very fierce battle was fought next to the wall. Egil, followed by his men, charged at the gate. Many townsmen were killed. They fell down one after the other. Egil was the first to go into the town and the other Vikings followed him. Some townspeople fled, but others were killed. Then Thorolf and his men plundered the town and took plenty of treasures. They set fire to the buildings before they left. Then they went back to their ships.

Egil's Saga tells of his adventures in Iceland, Norway, and England with his friend Thorolf. This passage tells of what happened on one adventure.

This is a picture of Egil Skallagrimsson from a seventeenth century manuscript of *Egil's Saga.* He was a *skald* as well as a warrior.

Music and dancing

There was music, but few **artifacts** have been found. Some sagas mention that Vikings played fiddles, pipes, and harps. They also enjoyed dancing to verse-singing, which was a kind of chanting.

Sports and Games

Hunting

Vikings loved hunting. They trained hawks, eagles, and falcons to kill wild birds and animals. They trained dogs to pick up whatever the hawks had killed.

Horses

Vikings hunted with horses. They also organized horse races and horse fights, where horses fought to the death.

Wrestling

Vikings enjoyed watching and taking part in wrestling. They wrestled on a field with a pointed stone in the middle. People stood around the edges to watch as the two wrestlers tried to force each other down onto the stone.

St. Olaf's **Saga** explains how a hawk and dogs were used to catch wild birds. This scene from a **tapestry** from 1092 shows how it might have been done.

Water sports

In the summer, Vikings rowed, sailed, and swam. They had competitions to see who could stay underwater the longest. In the winter, they skated and played ball games on frozen lakes and rivers. Vikings skied during the winter, too.

Summer sports

Vikings loved running, jumping, shooting with bows and arrows, fencing, rock climbing, and lifting heavy weights or stones. Balancing competitions were also very popular.

Games

Board games were very popular among the Vikings. In addition to chess, they also played a game that used dice and peg boards.

Many of these sports and games helped the Vikings to become strong. They needed strength and speed to survive in battle.

These are Viking chess pieces. Viking **traders** probably first saw chess played in Arabia and brought the game back with them.

The Port of Birka

Why was Birka important?

Birka was a Viking market town on an island in Lake Malar, Sweden. The town grew because it was where water routes from south and east met. It became a market town in about 800 C.E. and soon over 1,000 people were living there. **Archaeologists** have found evidence of industries such as leather working and bronze casting. They have found evidence of wooden houses, too. Birka was important to the Vikings. It is now important to archaeologists because from Birka they have learned how Viking ports grew.

Birka was a busy port throughout the year. In winter, **traders** crossed the frozen lake to trade furs. In summer, ships came to unload on the waterfront or in one of the three harbors.

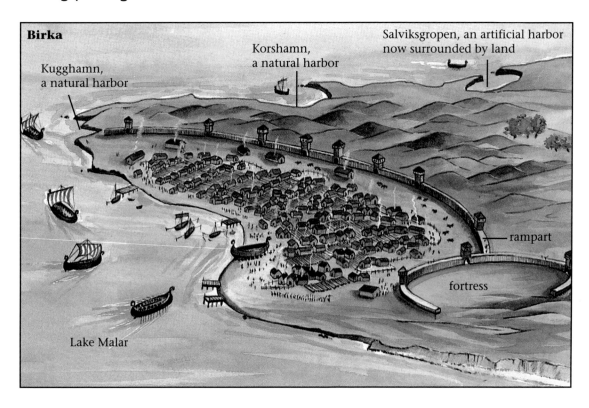

Birka

Kugghamn, a natural harbor

Korshamn, a natural harbor

Salviksgropen, an artificial harbor now surrounded by land

rampart

fortress

Lake Malar

This is an aerial view of modern Birka. The ramparts that bordered the trading center are still visible.

How did Viking ports grow?

Vikings sailed to other countries and traded with them. Viking traders needed markets in which to sell their goods. At first, the markets were temporary—stalls were set up and taken down every day. Gradually markets became more permanent. Towns began to grow around the markets. Craftworkers moved in. Vikings built warehouses for their goods and docks so that ships could be unloaded more easily. As market towns became richer, townspeople became afraid they would be attacked. So they built wooden stockades around their harbors and earth **ramparts** around their towns to protect against attack. Strong wooden fences were built on top of the ramparts with gates to allow people in and out.

Crafts and Craftworkers

Viking farmers made most of the things they and their families needed. Some goods, however, were made by special craftworkers. These craftworkers lived in large **trading** centers where there were plenty of people to buy their goods.

Metalworkers

Blacksmiths made tools and weapons from iron. Other metalworkers made jewelry from bronze, silver, and pewter.

Brooch makers

All Vikings wore brooches to fasten their cloaks, tunics, and **jerkins.** Vikings made brooches from bronze and pewter. Pewter brooches were cheaper than bronze brooches because the molds used to make them could be re-used.

This is part of a horse's harness. **Archaeologists** found it in Denmark. The metalwork is covered in a thin layer of gold. Vikings made patterns in the gold and cut hundreds of tiny notches to make the gold pattern sparkle in the light.

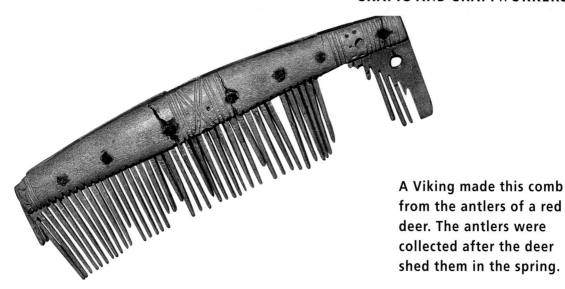

A Viking made this comb from the antlers of a red deer. The antlers were collected after the deer shed them in the spring.

Jewelry makers

Vikings made beads from **amber,** glass, and **jet** that they threaded into necklaces and bracelets. Pendants were made from amber or jet as well. They imported the glass from Germany and the jet from England.

Carvers

Vikings carved pins, spoons, and combs from deer antlers. Other carvers made wooden cups and bowls, barrels, and stools.

Leather workers

Leather workers made boots and shoes from the hides of animals.

Many of these goods were sold in the towns where they were made. Others were taken around to Viking settlements by traveling **merchants.**

Merchant Adventurers

Vikings traveled across the Atlantic Ocean and into the Mediterranean Sea. They sailed up the rivers of Russia and France. How do we know?

Runestones

Runestones tell of journeys made by the Vikings. There are Viking **runes** carved on a stone lion found in a Greek harbor. There are Viking runes carved in the Hagia Sophia church in Istanbul, Turkey.

Sagas

Sagas tell stories of **merchants** and their journeys. *Egil's Saga* tells about **trading** dried fish, skins, and furs for wheat, honey, wine, and cloth in England.

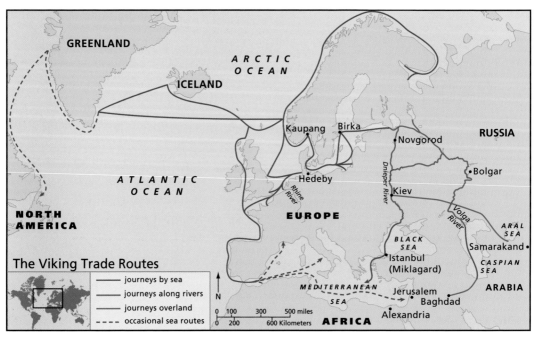

The Viking Trade Routes

journeys by sea
journeys along rivers
journeys overland
- - - - occasional sea routes

N

0 100   300   500 miles
0   200   600 Kilometers

Early on, Vikings did not have their own coins. Instead, they either swapped their goods for goods of equal value or weight, or used the silver in other people's coins to buy and sell.

Writings

Muslim writers Ibn Fadlan and Ibn Rustah wrote about slaves the Vikings transported along the Volga River to Istanbul, which the Vikings called Miklagard. In Miklagard markets, the slaves were exchanged for Arab silver and silks and spices from the east. King Alfred of Wessex, in England, wrote about the Viking who brought him bearskins, ropes made from walrus hide, and feathers for stuffing pillows and quilts.

Vikings did not always trade with foreigners. They traded with other Vikings in different parts of the world. Norwegian Vikings, for example, sent timber to Iceland, where there was little timber, in exchange for dried fish.

These weighing scales belonged to a Viking trader. Vikings bought and sold according to weight. Thus, traders had to carry scales around with them.

Travel and Transportation

Over sea, over land

Vikings preferred to travel on water, but not everywhere can be reached by boat. Overland travel in Denmark was easy because the Romans had left flat, straight roads. In Norway and Sweden, travel was difficult because of mountains and forests. Vikings built special roads across marshes. These roads were sometimes known as bridges. They put **runestones** beside them to say who had built these special roads. Near Hadeland, Sweden, there is a runestone that says "Gunnvor, Thirdrik's daughter, made this bridge in memory of her daughter, Astrid; she was the most skilful maiden in Hadeland."

During the winter, Vikings made skates from the foot bones of horses and cows. They tied these skates onto their boots with a strip of leather. They never lifted their feet, but pushed themselves over the snow with poles.

Traveling in winter

Traveling was easier during the winter. Lakes and rivers were frozen and the ground covered with ice and snow. Vikings skated from place to place. They used skis and snowshoes, too. They used sledges for carrying heavy loads over snow and ice.

This decorated Viking wagon belonged to a rich person. Ordinary Vikings used plain ones.

Traveling in summer

In summer, most Vikings walked from place to place. Only rich people went on horseback. Packhorses and wagons carried heavy loads where there were suitable roads. Vikings sometimes used special sledges that slid over grass when there were no roads.

This Viking **tapestry** shows wagons being pulled by horses. No one knows if this is a scene from everyday life or a special occasion. Whoever made the tapestry, though, probably based it on something they had seen.

Ships and Ship Building

Vikings were great sailors. When other Europeans were afraid to sail out of sight of land, the Vikings crossed the Atlantic Ocean. They also traveled long distances up rivers and landed their boats where there were no harbors.

A *faering* was a four-oared boat 21.3 feet (6.5 meters) long and 4.6 feet (1.4 meters) wide.

Vikings could do this because of the way their boats were designed. Their boats were long and slender, with a high curve at each end. They were light enough to sail in shallow water and strong enough to survive a storm. Large ships could be sailed or rowed. Small ships could be lifted over land from one river to another.

A *knarr* was used by **traders.** It was 49.2 feet (15 meters) long and 15.1 feet (4.6 meters) wide.

The Gokstad ship was 76.4 feet (23.3 meters) long and 16.4 feet (5 meters) wide. Vikings used longships like this for **raiding.**

The Oseberg burial ship was 70.8 feet (21.6 meters) long and 16.4 feet (5 meters) wide.

How do we know?

At first, people only knew about Viking ships from **sagas** and pictures carved in stone. Then, in 1880, **archaeologists** found a Viking longship buried in blue clay in Gokstad, Norway. They found another one in blue clay in Oseberg, Norway in 1903. The blue clay helped preserve the ships. In 1962, archaeologists found a *knarr,* a coastal trader, and a small fishing boat or ferry in Roskilde, Denmark. From these **excavations** they learned a lot about how Viking boats were built.

This is the Viking longship excavated from Gokstad, Norway in 1880. The body of a man was buried in it, along with his weapons and other belongings, including three small boats.

Building a Viking Longship

Vikings built their ships in winter when little other work could be done. They built them outside or sometimes in special boat sheds.

Choosing the wood

Vikings built longships from oak. They chose a tree trunk that was about 59 feet (18 meters) long for the **keel.** They chose tree trunks that were about 16 feet (5 meters) long for the wedge-shaped planks that were to be the sides of the ship.

Building the boat

First Vikings cut the keel. Then they nailed the front and back posts to it. Next, they added the planks, starting at the bottom and moving upwards. After this, they nailed the ribs, which held the ship in shape, onto the planks. Finally, a strong block of wood was fixed to the keel, in the middle of the ship, to support the mast.

The keel was the backbone of the ship. The end posts gave the ship its curved shape.

Timbers to make the frame and hold the ship in shape were added after the bottom planks were fixed in place.

Floor timbers were put on top of the frame and fastened to the planks with wooden pegs.

The mast block was fixed to the keel in the middle of the ship. It helped spread the weight of the mast evenly across the ship.

The rudder, like a large wooden paddle, was always fixed to the end of the ship.

Oar holes were cut into the top plank of the ship.

Clinker building

After the first line of planks were fastened into place, the second line was fastened above them. The wedge shape of the planks meant that they overlapped when they were nailed together. This is known as clinker building. Clinker building made the ship flexible and able to sail in heavy seas.

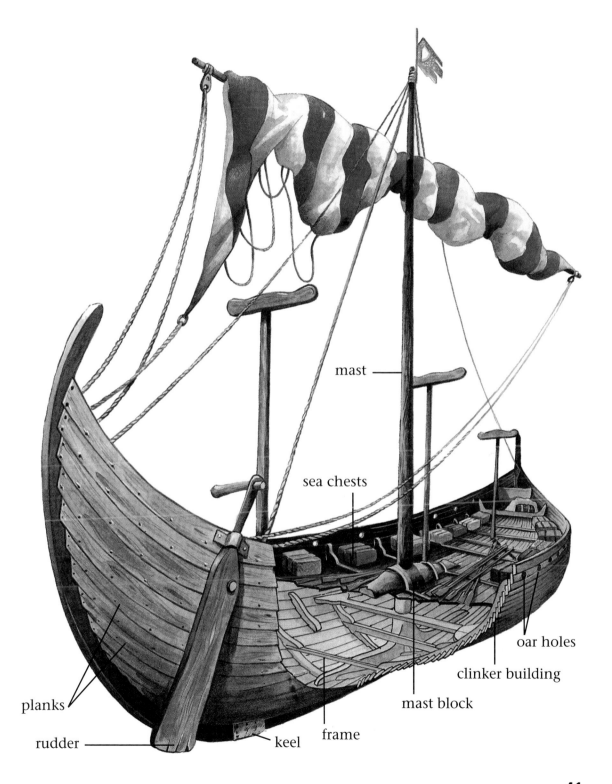

mast

sea chests

oar holes

clinker building

planks

mast block

rudder

frame

keel

Sailing and rowing

Vikings sailed their ships when the wind was strong enough and rowed them when it was not. They took wooden chests with them when they went to sea. These chests probably held their clothes and weapons. It is likely that Vikings sat on them when they rowed.

Food

Vikings stored food for the journey under the decks at each end of the longship. They took dried, smoked, or salted fish and meat, vats of butter and cheese, sacks of apples and nuts, as well as barrels of beer, water, and sour milk. On long voyages they mostly ate cold food. Cooking was sometimes done on the ship. The cooking fire was contained in a box so that the ship would not catch fire.

This is a weather vane. It was once fixed on the top of the mast of a Viking ship. Streamers and metal pendants would have been attached through the metal holes along the lower edge to blow and rattle in the wind.

Shelter

Vikings took large pieces of strong cloth with them and some tent posts. When their ships were in a harbor, the tent posts were put up on deck and the cloth stretched between them. This gave the Vikings shelter from the rain and sun. When the Vikings were sailing close to the shore, they sometimes anchored their ships for the night. Then they set up their tent shelters on the beach and brought their sleeping bags from the ship. They brought the ship's cooking pot, too, and had a hot meal.

Navigation

When they were out of sight of land, Vikings probably steered by the sun and stars. Viking navigators also relied on landmarks to find their way. Ravens were used by the Vikings as well. These birds were known for their ability to find land. If sailors were unsure about the direction of land, they would release a raven from the ship. Then they would sail in the same direction that the raven flew. Vikings would often pass directions on to each other.

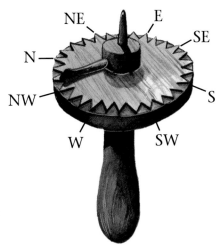

Vikings used bearing dials, like this drawing above and **artifact** below. The sun cast a shadow from the pin onto the dial. Then the Vikings knew the direction in which they were sailing.

Raiders and Traders

There are many reasons why some Vikings began to leave their homelands.

Too many people

In the 600s, Vikings cleared more and more land for farming. They produced more food. People were better fed and healthier than they had been in the past. More babies and children lived to be adults. This increase in people began to cause problems.

Not enough land

The eldest son in a Viking family inherited the family farm. The other sons had to make farms of their own by clearing more land. Soon,

These are two pages from the *Codex Aureus*, a manuscript stolen by the Vikings during a **raid** on Kent, England. A man named Earl Alfred paid the Vikings for the manuscript and brought it back to England.

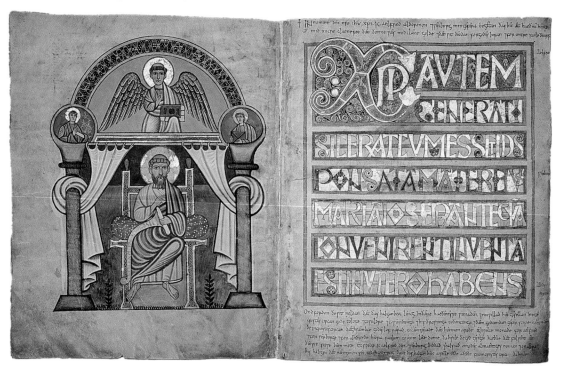

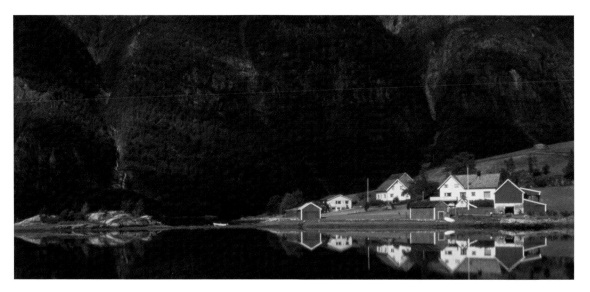

Vikings ran out of good land. Younger sons had to find other ways to make a living.

Viking traders

In the 700s, strong kings brought peace to the Vikings and their homelands. Vikings began to **trade** and transport more goods overseas. Some Vikings now became pirates and traders, instead of farmers.

Viking raiders

Some Vikings went **raiding.** In 787, Vikings raided Dorset, on the south coast of England. Six years later, on June 8, 793, they raided the **monastery** at Lindisfarne, on England's northeast coast. There they killed some of the **monks** and stole the monastery's treasures. This was just the beginning.

Although most Vikings were farmers, there was limited farmland in their homelands. In Norway, the only good farmland was along the sides of the **fjords,** as this picture shows. In Sweden, much of the land was either marshy or forested. In Denmark, there were large areas of sandy land where nothing would grow.

Viking Warriors

Vikings were fearless warriors. They often fought against much larger forces and relied on surprise in order to win.

Land battles

Vikings began battles by firing arrows at their enemies. Then they threw spears. After this, they hurled themselves at the enemy and began hand-to-hand fighting, using battle-axes and swords. If the other side began to win, the Vikings stood shoulder to shoulder and made a wall with their shields. Vikings at the back shot arrows high in the air, over the shield wall, at their enemies. Then they would start hand-to-hand fighting again.

Viking spears were metal points on top of long wooden poles. Spears were thrown at the beginning of the battle and picked up afterward.

Viking battle-axes had blades that were 9.5 inches (24 centimeters) wide. The blades were mounted on wooden shafts about 4.1 feet (1.25 meters) long.

Vikings made their swords from iron. Some swords were decorated with gold and silver.

Viking helmets were made from leather or iron. Their helmets fitted close to their heads and never had horns or wings attached.

Vikings made their shields from wood and iron.

Shirts made from thousands of iron rings linked together were called *byrnies.* Only Viking leaders could afford them.

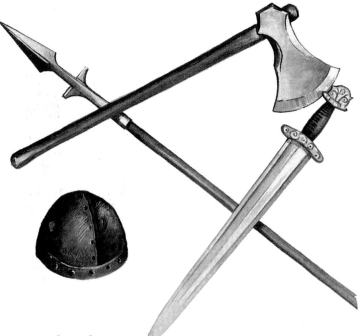

Viking warriors were buried with their weapons. They believed they would need them in **Valhalla.**

One of a Viking's most treasured possessions was his sword. Viking swords were made by twisting several iron rods together while they were very hot. Then they were hammered flat. The handle was also iron, but decorated with gold and silver.

Sea battles

Vikings tied their ships together so the enemy would not drive them apart. The chief warrior on each ship stood in the **prow** and fought until he fell. Then he was replaced. Often, these chief warriors were brave fighters called *berserkers.* These were fierce Vikings who were known to chew their shields, fight bare chested, and feel no pain. They supposedly were able to kill many men at one time.

Rewards

Usually Vikings shared any stolen treasure amongst themselves. Sometimes their enemies bribed the Vikings to go away. They paid them money called *Danegeld.* Vikings shared this amongst themselves, too.

The Vikings in England

Raiders and settlers

At first, the Vikings simply **raided** and destroyed English settlements. They made attacks and carried home whatever they had stolen. But in 850, for the first time, the Vikings stayed in England over the winter. In 865, they took *Danegeld* from the people who lived in Kent and in exchange promised to live there peacefully. The following year a great army of Vikings arrived in England, looking for land on which to settle. They conquered East Anglia and moved on to York, where they captured the city and crowned their own king. By 871, the whole country was in danger of attacks by Vikings.

The *Danelaw*

In 877, the Vikings attacked Wessex, the most powerful of England's seven kingdoms. Alfred, King of Wessex, defeated the Vikings. He made them promise to stay in one part of England, called the *Danelaw*. By 920, Alfred's son, Edward had recaptured the *Danelaw* and now there was one king over all England. The Vikings continued to fight back. In 1013, Sweyn Forkbeard, King of Denmark, defeated the English King Ethelred and gained England. Sweyn died a few weeks later.

There are many Viking crosses in cemeteries in northern England. This is a Viking cross in a cemetery in Gosforth, England. It shows scenes from both Christian and Viking religions.

THE VIKINGS IN ENGLAND

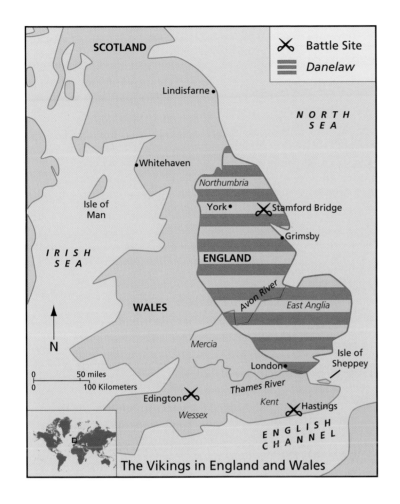

The Vikings in England and Wales

This **runestone** from Uppland, Sweden tells of Ulf, who "received *Danegeld* three times in England."

The end of the raids

After Ethelred's death in 1016, Sweyn's son, Canute ruled Norway, England, and Denmark. But when his son died in 1042, the English chose Ethelred's son to be their king. The last Viking attack on England was led by the Norwegian Harald Hardradi in 1066. He was defeated at Stamford Bridge. William of Normandy became king and the Viking raids ended.

Scotland and Ireland

Scotland

Archaeologists have discovered from their **excavations** that, by 800, several Norwegian Viking families had settled in the Orkney and Shetland Islands. They **raided** the islands of Skye and Iona. Some moved on to the Scottish mainland and settled there.

Ireland

Vikings from Scotland raided Ireland. At first they raided **monasteries** on the coast, but by 830 they were sailing up the rivers to raid towns inland. In 841, Vikings began building bases, called *long-phorts.* They built *long-phorts* at Dublin, Limerick, Wexford, Waterford, and Cork. They used these bases to fight off raids from other Vikings, as well as attacks by the Irish. In 851, these Norwegian Vikings were defeated by a force

This is a picture of a modern Up-Helly-Aa. This is a festival held every year in Lerwick, Shetland (Scotland). The festival remembers when the Shetland Islands belonged to Norway.

The Vikings in Scotland and Ireland

Legend:
- places where the Vikings settled
- ✗ battle site
- ■ *long-phorts*

Shetland Island — Jarlshof
Orkney Island
Hebrides
Skye
SCOTLAND
Iona
NORTH SEA
ATLANTIC OCEAN
IRELAND
Tara ✗
Clontarf ✗
■ Dublin
Isle of Man
■ Limerick
■ Wexford
Cork ■ Waterford
WALES
ENGLAND

0   50   100 miles
0   100 Kilometers

N

of Danish Vikings and Irishmen. Later in the year, the Norwegians recaptured Dublin and stayed there until 902, when the Irish defeated them again. In 917 the Vikings were back, and turned Dublin into a busy and prosperous port.

Tara and Clontarf

The Vikings were defeated by the Irish at Tara in 980 and at Clontarf in 1014. But they were allowed to stay in Ireland because they were skilled **traders** and their towns were very wealthy. Then, in 1170, an army attacked Dublin. These new invaders were Normans, whose families had settled in England 100 years before.

France and the Mediterranean

Trading and raiding

Between 768 and 814, King Charlemagne ruled France and most of western Europe. Vikings **traded** with parts of his **empire.** Then, in 810 when the empire began to crumble, they began **raiding** it. In 845 Vikings attacked Paris. The French king paid the Vikings 6,615 pounds (3,000 kilograms) of silver to go away. In the same year, Vikings reached Hamburg, Germany.

Settling

At the same time, Vikings from Scotland were attacking the Atlantic coast of France. In 835, they raided the French **monastery** at

In 844, Vikings attacked northwest Spain and then sailed south. This painting shows Muslim soldiers in Spain defeating the Vikings at Cordoba. These soldiers were the first to defeat a large number of Vikings.

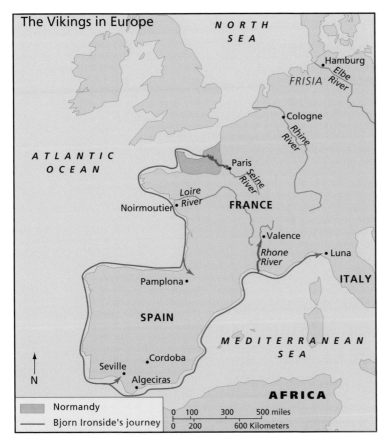

The Vikings in Europe

In 859, Bjorn Ironside and Hastein were forced to leave their base in France. They took 62 ships filled with gold, slaves, and food and headed toward Spain. The pink line on the map shows where they went. They raided, burned, and looted in Spain, France, Italy, and North Africa. After six years, they returned to France with their loot and only twenty ships left.

Noirmoutier. By 843, the **monks** had left and the Vikings were using Noirmoutier as their winter base.

Rollo and Normandy

The French paid more and more *Danegeld* to the Vikings, but they still kept raiding. Then, in 911 the King of France had a good idea. He made a Viking king named Rollo the Duke of Normandy. In exchange, Rollo became a Christian and promised to defend Normandy against other Vikings. Rollo and his men settled in Normandy.

New Lands to the West

Iceland

Vikings from Norway first went to Iceland in about 860. Floki, possibly the first Viking to see Iceland, gave the island its name. The Vikings probably arrived in Iceland by accident because of a storm. Irish **monks** were already living there when the Vikings arrived. They fled because they did not want to live anywhere near the Vikings.

Greenland

Around 985, Vikings from Iceland settled in Greenland. They took animals with them, but corn, iron, and timber had to be imported. All went well for 200 years. Then the climate got colder. Ice made the sea dangerous and **merchants** stopped visiting. Disease started to spread, and by 1500 the farms were deserted.

This is a reconstruction at L'Anse aux Meadows in Newfoundland of the first Viking **site** found in North America. There have been many attempts to fake Viking existence in North America. For example, a **runestone** in Kensington, Minnesota, found in 1898 was proved to be a fake in 1958.

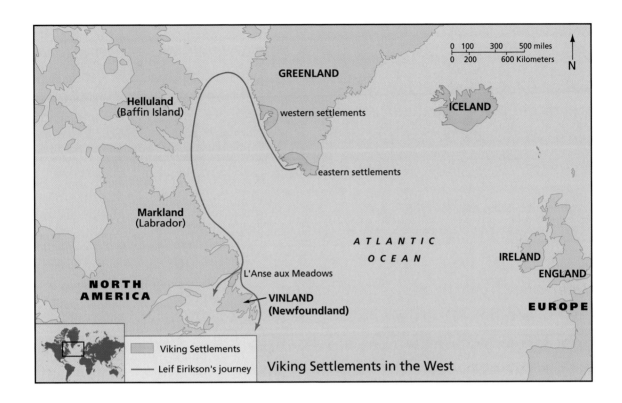

Viking Settlements in the West

North America

In about 985, a Viking named Bjarni Herjolfsson
was blown off course and was the first to see
the coast of North America. He did not land,
but returned to Greenland and told the Vikings
what he had seen. Leif Eirikson went looking
for this new land. He went first to Helluland,
then Markland, and finally to Vinland. He
stayed there for one winter and returned to
Greenland in the spring. The following year,
his brother Thorwald went and was killed by
Native Americans.

Trade Routes to the East

Around 860, Vikings from Sweden went east to Russia. The area was already inhabited by tribes of Slavs who lived by farming, hunting, and **trading.** The Slavs built a huge trading center at Ladoga, in Russia. Vikings used it as a base for trade routes deep inland.

Ladoga to Baghdad

Vikings sailed along the Volga River to Bolgar. Bolgar was an important overland trade route from the east. There they traded their slaves, honey, furs, and wax for silver from Arabia and silk from China. Some Vikings sailed on, down the Volga River and across the Caspian Sea. Then they left their boats and went by camel to Baghdad (in modern Iraq). They traded there for silks, silver, and spices.

Ladoga to Istanbul

Vikings sailed south along the Volkhov River to Novgorod, another great trading center. Then they sailed down the Dnieper River to Kiev, and on across the Black Sea to Istanbul (in modern Turkey). There they traded their goods for spices, wine, silks, and jewelry. Most traders made their way back up the rivers to Birka in Sweden.

This **runestone** is in Broby, Sweden. It was put up by Estrid in memory of her husband. It says: "He visited Jerusalem and died in Greece."

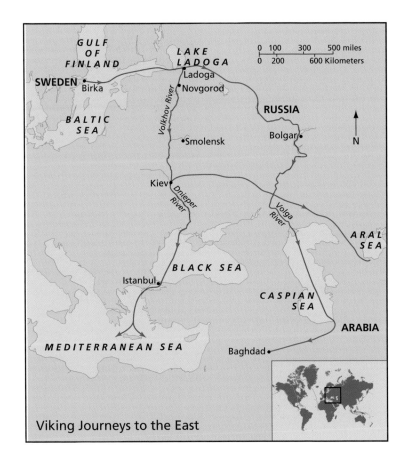

Viking Journeys to the East

Vikings who didn't go home

Some Vikings stayed in Istanbul. They joined the Varangian Guard. These were the Viking soldiers who guarded the emperor in Istanbul. One of the most famous of these soldiers was named Harald Sigurdson. Later, he became Harald Hardradi, King of Norway (1046–66). In 1066, he attacked England but was defeated by Harold Godwinson at the Battle of Stamford Bridge.

These **artifacts** are from a Viking settlement. Objects made by Vikings have been found at Kiev and Smolensk. A Viking from Sweden named Rurik gave Russia its name since the Slav name for Viking was *Rus.*

The Viking Sunset

The Viking Age lasted for about 300 years. There were several reasons why it ended.

Christianity

Denmark and then Norway were converted to Christianity. Sweden kept to the old religion the longest, but eventually converted as well. A Norwegian king, Olaf Haraldsson, converted many of his people to Christianity. He became known as Saint Olaf because people said that miracles happened at his grave. Many Vikings were forced to become Christians.

This Viking smith's mold could make Christian crosses and Thor's hammers. The two religions carried on side by side for a long time. Many Viking **traders** became Christians because it made it easier to deal with others who were already Christians.

Farming

Better farming methods improved the Vikings' homelands. More land was brought into use. Younger sons could now get farms without moving overseas.

Marriage

Vikings settled in places like **Danelaw,** Russia, and Ireland. There, they married and mixed with the local people.

Defeats

Raiding began to fail because people were prepared for the Vikings and defeated them.

Trade

Merchants began trading in bulky goods
and not in luxury goods. They needed bigger
ships that could carry bulky cargo.

The Viking legacy

The Vikings left behind the idea of laws. The
word "law" is Viking. Also, Vikings were the
first to use a jury of twelve men to decide
who was right or wrong in a dispute.

This wooden church
is in Borgund on the
Sognefjord, Norway.
It was built in the 1100s
and 1200s. The Viking
Age was over, but Viking
dragons as well as
crosses were used on
the roof.

Time Line

789   Vikings land on the south coast of England.

793   Vikings **raid** the **monastery** at Lindisfarne, an island off the northeast coast of England.

795   Vikings raid the Scottish island of Iona and make first raids on Ireland.

800   Vikings begin to settle in the Orkney and Shetland islands.

810   Danish Vikings raid Frisia.

834   Vikings raid the market town of Dorestad in the Netherlands.

835   Fifteen years of Viking raids on England begin.

841   Vikings build first *long-phort* in Dublin, Ireland.

844   Vikings reach Spain for the first time and are defeated by the Arabs.

845   Vikings besiege Paris and are bought off with *Danegeld.*

850   Vikings spend the winter in England for the first time and Swedish Vikings start to visit Russia.

860   Iceland is discovered by Norwegian Vikings and Swedish Vikings attack Istanbul (in modern Turkey).

874   The first Vikings settle in Iceland.

878   Alfred the Great, King of Wessex in England, defeats the Vikings at the Battle of Edington.

886   Danish Vikings settle in the English *Danelaw.*

911   Viking king Rollo settles in Normandy, France, at the invitation of the French king.

930   The first *Althing* held in Iceland, where 10,000 Vikings are living.

980   Christianity starts to spread through the Viking homelands.

982   Eirik the Red sails from Iceland and reaches Greenland.

986   Bjarni Herjolfsson sees Vinland (Newfoundland), but does not land.

1000   People in Iceland accept Christianity.

1002   Leif Eirikson sails from Greenland and reaches Vinland.

1014   At the Battle of Clontarf the Irish king, Brian Boru, defeats the Vikings in Ireland.

1016   Danish Vikings defeat the English at the Battle of Ashington. Sweyn Forkbeard becomes king of England, followed by his son, Canute.

1042   Canute's son, Harthacanute, dies and the English choose Edward the Confessor to be king of England.

1047   Harald Hardradi becomes king of Norway.

1066   Edward the Confessor dies. Harold Godwinson becomes king of England. Harald Hardradi invades northern England and is defeated by Harold Godwinson. Duke William of Normandy invades southern England and defeats Harold Godwinson at the Battle of Hastings. Viking raids on England end.

1100   The Viking Age ends.

Glossary

amber hard, yellowish to brownish substance that is the fossilized resin of trees buried thousands of years ago

archaeologist person who learns about life in the past by looking for and studying objects from earlier times

artifact object made by people

Danegeld money paid by people to the Vikings in order to be left in peace

Danelaw part of England given to the Vikings by King Alfred the Great after they were defeated. It included East Anglia and five main towns: Derby, Leicester, Lincoln, Nottingham, and Stamford.

empire group of countries that come under the control of one ruling country

excavation careful digging up of buried objects to find out about the past

fertile able to grow many crops

feud long-lasting and violent fighting between two families

fjord narrow section of the sea between cliffs or steep slopes

fodder plants grown for animal feed

historian someone who finds out about the past by studying different written and printed documents

jarl rich Viking landowner

jerkin hip-length sleeveless jacket

jet hard, black material like coal but clean and shiny

karl free-born Viking

keel main piece of wood that goes along the bottom of a ship from end to end

longhouse Viking farmhouse that got its name because of its long, narrow shape

long-phort one of the places in Ireland where the Vikings first stayed over winter. Later, they developed into trading towns.

mead alcoholic drink made from honey

merchant person who buys and sells goods

monastery place where monks live and practice their religion

monk member of a religious group of men who live in monasteries away from the rest of the world

noble person born into an important family

prow front part of a ship

raider person who makes short, surprise attacks on other people and their property; to make short, surprise attacks is to raid

rampart bank of earth built around a town to protect it from attackers

rune one of the marks or letters used to write down the Viking language. They were straight and stick-like, which made them easy to carve.

runestone stone with Viking runes carved on it

saga long and detailed Viking story about their adventures

settler person who has left their own homeland to live in a new area or country

site area on the ground where there was once a building and that archaeologists are excavating

tapestry picture or design embroidered on canvas using different colored wool

Thing open-air meeting of Vikings to settle arguments and discuss problems

thrall Viking slave

trader person who makes a living by buying and selling goods; to buy and sell goods is to trade

Valhalla final home or paradise where Viking warriors went after they died

vellum specially prepared skin, usually of a calf, on which the Vikings wrote

More Books to Read

Burgan, Michael. *Leif Eriksson.* Chicago: Heinemann Library, 2002.

Finney, Fred. *Viking Longboat.* Brookfield, Conn.: Millbrook Press, 1997.

Grant, Neil. *The Vikings.* Cary, N.C.: Oxford University Press, 1998.

Index